EIGHT KEYS
TO
SUCCESS

EIGHT KEYS
— TO —
SUCCESS

by
Jim Bakker

Edited by
Jeffrey Park

PTL TELEVISION NETWORK
CHARLOTTE, NC 28279

© 1980 by
Heritage Village Church &
Missionary Fellowship, Inc.
Charlotte, NC 28279
All rights reserved
Printed in the United States

All scriptures in King James Version unless otherwise noted.

Library of Congress No. 79-92249
ISBN: 0-89221-071-0

New Leaf Press
P.O. Box 1045 Harrison, Ar. 72601   741-2514

"This book of the Law shall not depart out of thy mouth; but thou shalt meditate therein day and night, that thou mayest observe to do according to all that is written therein: for then thou shalt make thy way prosperous, and then thou shalt have good success."

JOSHUA 1:8

Dear PTL Friend,

It doesn't take extraordinary insight to see that we live in a world of spiritual confusion, emotional upheaval and great mental pressure. Perhaps the greatest struggle in our society today is that personal striving to be successful in our own eyes as well as those of our peers.

Through nineteen years of active ministry, I have discovered that success is not a goal, but rather a by-product of walking in the will of God. There are, however, certain God-given keys that will help us move into and stay in the will of God which will insure successful and abundant living for each of us. In the following eight messages, I share some of these that have changed my life and kept me in His path.

My prayer is that you will grow in God's grace and love and receive His rich blessings upon you daily.

In Warmest Christian Love,

Jim Bakker

CONTENTS

1 Learn To Lean On Jesus

The week of August 8-13, 1977, Jim Bakker and the PTL staff took the PTL Club on location to Mount Union, Pennsylvania for a PTL Family Camp-in and the Jesus '77 rally. Nearly twenty thousand enthusiastic campers gathered to hear Jim give the following message during Jesus '77.

Every week we have thousands of our PTL Partners and friends who come to visit us in Charlotte to see the "live" programming of the PTL Club. When our Partners see the miracle that God has performed in putting together all the beautiful facilities at Heritage Village, many come up to me and seem to want to put Jim Bakker on a pedestal. They ask, "How did you get all this faith?" Or comment, "How come you are so successful? Jim, you must really be something special for God to do all this through you."

When they say those things, I just have to answer them, "Yes, God has made me special. I'm special because I'm a King's kid. And as one of God's children, so are you."

God desires that each of us be successful. He wants to work supernaturally through each of us. He will, too, as we learn to lean on His power and strength. The whole ministry of PTL has been built out of God giving me some simple principles from His Word that have taught me how to lean on Jesus. These principles are found in Psalm 37, verses three through seven: "TRUST in the Lord, and do good; so shalt thou dwell in the land, and verily thou shalt be fed. DELIGHT thyself also in the Lord; and he shall give thee the desires of thine heart. COMMIT thy way unto the Lord; trust also in him; and he shall bring it to pass. And he shall bring forth thy righteousness as the light, and thy judgment as the noonday. REST in the Lord, and wait patiently for him: fret not thyself because of him who prospereth in his way, because of the man who bringeth wicked devices to pass."

Before we continue, let's pray together:

Father, I pray you'll be with us . . . God, give some words to speak that will change our lives together and challenge our hearts. Anoint our ears as we listen and our lips as we speak. Meet every need of every person. We're your people God and we need You every day. We can't do anything without You, Lord. God, be with us now in the name of Jesus. Amen.

The truths found in these five verses we just read have given me, and can give you, a supernatural faith in God.

1. TRUST in the Lord and do good (vs.3).

The primary meaning of the Hebrew word, translated trust, is "to move toward a place of refuge." This is the first and primary step in both salvation and learning to lean on Jesus. Before a person can be saved, he must first recognize his need to be saved.

This world is no place of refuge for a Christian. Overnight, without warning, our earthly riches can vanish, our health can be taken away and our physical lives destroyed. Our only hope is to move to a place of greater refuge. God is that refuge — His word is sure and constant. Though others fail and deceive us, God is faithful to His promises. I have heard many people argue about things in the Bible, but I've never heard any say God's Word doesn't work. God is faithful!

Learning to trust God isn't something that happens overnight. It is something that you learn one step at a time. Several years ago, it took every ounce of my faith to trust God for $200/monthly. Now our budget is nearly four million dollars monthly. But you start where you are and as you see God's faithfulness, you learn to trust God more. If you feel you have no faith, get around people who do. It will encourage you. The key to learning to "trust" is to "try." We must start to move. Just like the guidance system of a missile, which isn't activated until it is launched, we will never develop confidence in God until we try Him.

2. DELIGHT yourself in the Lord (vs. 4).

This word, delight, speaks of confessing confidence in God. It means literally to be pliable and open up, to express one's appreciation. When we receive a wonderful gift or see something beautiful, what is the first thing we want to do? We want to tell others all about it. This is what delighting in the Lord is all about.

Proverbs 18:21 tells us that death and life are in the power of the tongue. By our confession, we can choose our future. Most of us are quick to acknowledge our needs and our problems, but there is no life in that. The Bible tells us rather to acknowledge God in all our ways. He is the answer. Just as God in creation spoke all the heaven and earth into existence, we can speak abundance and prosperity and blessing into existence by delighting in God and confessing His answer.

Several years ago we by faith spoke the Heritage Village before God; today it is complete and totally paid for — simply because we spoke with delight the desires of our heart before God. Of course, we then worked night and day to bring our faith in line with God's Word. But it started first with speaking the word of faith; God always honors a good confession of faith.

3. COMMIT your way unto the Lord (vs. 5).

Commit comes from the Hebrew primal root, galal, meaning "roll into." It has the connotations of deep involvement and is translated elsewhere as "roll together" and even "wallow." This is committing our way unto the Lord — becoming so involved with Christ that we are rolled (moved) together with Him.

How do we commit our way to the Lord? We start by setting priorities. If God is to be first in our lives, then what we commit to God must also be first in our lives — our time, our talent and our money.

The reason that some Christians never come to this place of commitment is that they always have a plan B. "If the Lord doesn't provide, I'll do this." Or "If God doesn't heal me, I'll do that." This is not committed faith so they wind up with plan B. People who come to work at PTL with a plan B don't last long. Praise God, most of them get converted to committed faith.

I know a person is getting serious with God when I see him or her setting aside a prime time in the day to get apart with God to pray. God requires our time to be able to commit His will to us. When PTL first started, God showed me that if we were to do God's will, it would require constant prayer. Today members of our staff set aside work time to maintain a constant\ prayer vigil in our intercessory prayer chapel for the needs of the ministry and our Partners.

God requires our talents so that His will can flow through us. I believe that PTL has the most talented staff in the world. Yet many couldn't find a job before coming to PTL. The difference? They started delighting in God and in His power. Then God revealed their talents and ambitions.

God also requires our money, so His will can multiply in us. A Christian who does not give God his tithe and more is like the farmer who eats his seed before he plants it. God will bless and multiply everything we commit to Him. That is why I enjoy giving to other ministries, it always comes back multiplied by God.

4. REST in the Lord and WAIT patiently for Him (vs 7).

There are really two sides of one principle that describe our leaning on Jesus and which result from trusting, delighting and committing. One side is the "rest" from the Hebrew "daman," meaning to be dumb, to quiet self, to stand still. This is our reaction to our enemies. We just turn dumb to the fear, bitterness and resentment that arise when circumstances or other people come against us. When we fight back or judge others, we only get the same judgment back on ourselves. Rest means to let God fight our battles. He can do it better. If we fear or try to fight our enemies, we become slaves to them. If we commit them to God and rest, He will thrust them out — even turning them into friends. Many people have called me and have apologized for things that they have said against me, because God has fought my battles when I wouldn't get involved and just committed them to God.

The other side of rest is to "wait patiently." The Hebrew word here, "Chiyl," means literally to twist or intertwine. It was used to describe the process by which the Hebrew women made a strong rope by twisting together four strands of hemp.

Waiting on the Lord, therefore, is not a passive thing but an active expectancy of involving oneself with God to bring about His will. Solomon describes this in Ecclesiastes 4:12: "If one prevail against him, two shall withstand him, and a threefold cord is not quickly broken."

As our little cord of faith becomes intertwined with the cords of the Father, Son and Holy Spirit, suddenly it takes on a great new strength and power that accomplishes the impossible every time. This is leaning on Jesus.

In the Song of Solomon (8:5) we see a beautiful picture of this in the words, "Who is this that comes up from the wilderness leaning on her beloved?" Have you been in the wilderness of struggle and trial? Come to Jesus and lean on His strength. He will bring you out to a place of success and victory!

2 Give A Good Report

At the 1977 World Convention, of the Full Gospel Business Men's Fellowship International, Jim Bakker spoke to an overflow crowd of more than 7000 people gathered at the Conrad Hilton Hotel in Chicago.

I believe God is more concerned about what we say than anything else we do. That may sound surprising, but it is Bible.

Do you know that where you spend eternity is determined by your confession? Romans chapter 10, verses 9 and 10, tell me that if I confess the Lordship of Jesus Christ and believe on His name, I will be saved. And Jesus tells me in the Gospel of Luke, chapter 19 and verse 22, that the judgment of the wicked will come from the words of their own mouths.

Your future, your success, your testimony, your

very life is governed by your confession. In the book of Proverbs, Chapter 18 and verse 21, we read: "Death and life are in the power of the tongue: and they that love it shall eat the fruit thereof."

Let us pray together.

Heavenly Father, I ask you now to bless these scriptures and these words which you have given to me to bring to these people. God, I pray for unity in the Body of Christ, that the prayer of Jesus Christ will be answered, that we will be one, that the world will see Jesus. And Lord, we'll give you the praise and the glory and the honor. In Jesus name, I pray. Amen."

Speech is undoubtedly one of the most powerful forces on this earth. God, Himself, spoke the entire universe into being. In creation, He gave man the power to speak and the ability to choose what to say, whether good or evil. While our speech is by choice, for a Christian, a good confession is not an option, it is a necessity.

I believe the thing that has kept Christianity back from success and total victory in this world is a bad and negative confession.

We have all met people, even in our churches, who are always negative: their kids are sick; their job is rotten; this has gone wrong; the weather is bad; they always seem miserable. Their own confession has put them in a negative realm in which they will stay until they confess God's word and give a good report.

Each of us has the opportunity to change our life by our confession. Matthew 12:37 says that by our words, we will be justified or condemned. In fact, Jesus in the same conversation, says that a Christian can be known by the fruit of his lips just as a good tree is known by its fruit. Therefore, I really question whether a person is a Christian who is negative all the time.

For many, their degree of success, the condition of their home, their family, their business and their health is a direct result of their confession. We can confess doom or prosperity. Doctors have learned recently that our body will work to keep us honest to our confession. If we confess fear, our body responds and produces it, sometimes to the point oï heart failure (Luke 22:26). If we confess complaints and bitterness, our body will produce it in arthritis, cancer, etc. However, we can also confess a good report and our body will produce healing, life and prosperity.

Proverbs 15:30, one of Henry Harrison's (my co-host) favorite scriptures says, "a good report makes the bones fat." The Hebrew literally says, "a good report refreshes the whole body and causes the whole body to prosper." This is not only true in the physical realm but also in the spiritual. As we give a good report, a good testimony, we help the whole Body of Christ. I believe this is the reason that God has so blessed PTL's venture into 24 hours-a-day satellite broadcasting around the world. Instead of beaming violence and evil, it is airing a good report of Christian testimony and music 24 hours a day, not just using PTL's programs, but programs from all the leading Christian ministries, all working together, causing the whole Body to prosper.

GOD LOVES GOOD REPORTS

God loves a good report. Hebrews, chapter 11 is like a Christian Hall of Fame. It is a record of those men that gave a good report (vs 39) and who confessed they were looking for a better land (vs 14). For most, their circumstances were worse than yours or mine, but because they gave a good report, God honored them above measure.

The book of Job is a clear testimony of how to get out of a bad situation by giving a good report. If there ever was a situation where a person had a right to give a bad report, it was Job's. God tested Job by allowing the devil to afflict him, so even his wife suggested he "curse God and die." But the Bible says that Job did not sin with his lips. He could look in faith beyond his present adverse circumstances to see in nature and his own experience God's greatness and goodness. So when Job prayed for his three backbiting neighbors, God restored all his blessings and made Job the most blessed man on earth at that time.

Our present bad situation may be trying to keep us from making a good confession. Forget the circumstances; let's look up to God. The Bible says, "let the weak say, I am strong" (Joel 3:10). We can change our husband or wife, our business, our church, our pastor, all by a good confession. Just as we see everything in the Bible is positive when we see it in its proper context, all things are working together for our good when we confess good things.

Hebrews 10:23 tells us "to hold fast to our profession of faith without wavering." That means we must speak it forth. I enjoy sharing my faith in Jesus everyday on national television because I know as I confess Christ, He is confessing me before the Father.

GOD HATES EVIL REPORTS

Just as God loves a good report, He hates an evil

report. We can see this clearly in God's Word. In Numbers 13, we see the children of Israel preparing to cross Jordan to go over to the promised land. But Moses, first, sends twelve spies into the land to bring back a report. When they return, ten of the twelve bring back an evil report. Instead of confessing God's power and the goodness of the land, they speak of giants, walled cities and great enemies in the land (vs 32).

What was the result of their evil report? The Israelites started murmuring against God and decided that slavery in Egypt would be better, even after they had seen so many miracles of God. There are churches today that have been wiped out or have fallen into spiritual bondage by one evil report, gossip or backbiting. God was so upset with the spies' evil report that He determined to smite them with pestilence and disinherit them. Those who gave the evil report indeed died on the spot by a plague (Numbers 14:37). A plague of death also fell upon Ananias and Sapphira in Acts 5 because of their sinful, lying confession, despite the fact they had done a good deed.

GOOD REPORT IS TITLE DEED

What about the two spies, Joshua and Caleb, who gave the good report? Because of their positive trusting confession, they were almost stoned by a mob of their own people. But God honored them and promised that they alone of their whole generation would enter and possess the promised land (Numbers 14:24). God honored their *confession* of faith as a title deed to Canaan, more than if they had worked years to earn it.

Today, God will honor our confession of faith in the same way. When God gave us the idea for Heritage Village, we had no money and no visible means to get any. But we confessed it before God and man, and God has honored that confession. Today, Heritage Village is built and totally paid for.

If we as Christians only knew the power we have in our tongue to produce life, prosperity and Christian victory, I believe we would take the world for Christ this very year. John, in Revelation, chapter 12, saw the devil cast out of heaven to earth to try to deceive the saints. But the saints overcame him! How? By the blood of the Lamb and the word of their testimony! We don't have to fight the devil. We have more power on the tip of our tongue than the whole devil's army. All we have to do is confess God's Word and tell the devil to get lost. The scripture says, "Greater is He that is in us than he that is in the world. We are more than conquerors in Jesus. Whosoever is born of God overcomes the world."

This is our good report. This is the confession that is bigger than any problem the enemy can throw at us. As we confess God's goodness and power and love, it is our title to success and every one of God's promises and privileges in His Kingdom. Amen!

3 Start Loving Now

On May 13, 1978, nearly sixty thousand Christians of all different denominations gathered at Meadowlands Stadium in Rutherford, New Jersey to proclaim "Jesus Is Lord." The New York Times described the gathering as "one of the largest meetings of Charismatic Christians ever held in the United States."

Heavenly Father, I pray now that You anoint every ear that hears (and every person that reads this book). God, grant me a miracle. Don't let one person in this great coliseum (or who reads this book) miss heaven. But God, may everyone be a caring member of the Body of Jesus Christ. God, let the world see the love of God demonstrated — not just talked about, but acted upon. In the name of Jesus Christ of Nazareth I pray. Amen.

At the heart of any successful person, organization or church is a willingness to love. I now want to share with you a subject that I call, "Love Is Now." Let's look into John 17:21-23: "That they all may be one; as thou, Father, art in me, and I in thee, that they also may be one in us: that the world may believe that thou hast sent me. And the glory which thou gavest me I have given them; I in them, and thou in me, that they may be made perfect in one; and that the world may know that thou hast sent me, and hast loved them, as thou hast loved me."

As a young man, I had the privilege of sitting at the feet of a wonderful pastor and his wife. Sister Olson would teach me all about the love of God. As she taught me she would make Jesus so real that tears would stream down my face. Then I would pray, "Oh, God, my prayer is that someday I can make the love of God real to people." Today, I believe the world is still hungry for that kind of love.

COMBING THE WORLD FOR LOST SOULS

Sister Olson also began to share a message about Jesus, where she called Him "God's beachcomber." The beachcomber walks the shores of the beach and picks up bits of wrecked ships and pieces of wood in which nobody else can see any beauty. But the beachcomber picks up those old pieces of wrecked ships and makes something beautiful out of them.

"Jesus was God's beachcomber," she continued, "walking the shores of this old world, picking up wrecked lives and putting the pieces back together again, loving the unlovely, loving those whom nobody else cares about."

I want you to know that Jesus, right now, is walk-

ing all around this land with outstretched arms saying, "Come unto me all ye that labor and are heavy
laden." I believe in this hour it is the job of the Church
of Jesus Christ to love now, to reach out now to a sick
and dying world! 2 Corinthians 6:2 says: "Behold, now
is the accepted time; behold, now is the day of Salvation."

A message that God is speaking loud and clear to
the Church today is that we must love one another;
that the Charismatics love the non-Charismatics; that
the black love the white and the white love the black;
that we reach out to love the unlovely; and that we
love those of different denominations.

Our unity is a sign of Jesus' coming. One of the
most exciting things that I have ever experienced is to
minister with my Spirit-filled Catholic brothers and
sisters in various meetings and rallies. This happening is a sign of the soon return of Jesus Christ, as God
says to us in Hebrews 10:24: "Not forsaking the
assembling of ourselves together, as the manner of
some is; but exhorting one another: and so much the
more, as ye see the day approaching."

I asked God how we would be protected in these
last days. What would be our protection? What
should we do as the Body of Christ? He said, "My
Church will take care of itself. Get together and begin
to love one another. Your strength will be in the unity
of the Body of Christ."

When movie stars get together, they all give each
other awards. Recently, I watched a roast on television and I got to thinking, "How could we Christian
leaders all get together and honor any one member?"
It would be difficult just to get a group of people
together; and then, who would we honor? I thought of
one man who had been in the ministry for a long time

and so I felt he would be good. Then I thought, "Who would come?" You know, the movie stars all give awards to one another, and they seem to love each other. How much more should the Church of Jesus Christ begin to get together! Politicians get together and they don't even trust each other. Fraternities — they all get together. One time I stopped at a hotel where a group of young doctors, who had gone to college together, were gathered having a good time. They hadn't forgotten each other.

I wonder how many times we as Christians have forgotten one another. The Body of Christ needs to care now! Here is what the Word says in 1 Corinthians 12:25-26: "That there should be no schism in the body; but that the members should have the same care one for another. And whether one member suffers, all the members suffer with it; or one member be honored, all the members rejoice with it."

That is God's word. And again in John 13:34-35, we read,"A new commandment I give unto you, That ye love one another; as I have loved you, that ye also love one another. By this shall all men know that ye are my disciples, if ye have love one to another."

This very meeting, I believe, will bring hundreds and thousands of people to the feet of Jesus and to the foot of the cross; not by anything basically that has been done here, but by the very demonstration of love. If we are going to love each other, do it now! Don't say you are going to do it in the future, because the future doesn't come. Do it now!

LOVE REAPS LOVE

Beloved, if God so loved us, we ought also to love one another. Your Christian love will change lives.

Your Christian love will transform others.

When I was living in California, a family began to watch the PTL Club. That family had not been out of their home for several years because they were overweight and embarrassed to go out into the public. They began to watch the PTL Club, and somehow the love of God came through the program into their living room. They began to call us and write us. Tammy and I began to take them out for drives. This was the first time in several years they had come out of their own home. They were so embarrassed because they were overweight and afraid people would laugh at them. Love began to change their lives.

The scriptures tell us that, "Bread cast upon the waters shall return after many days." Well, there soon was a time when we were in desperate need. I had nowhere to turn and no income. It was the lady and her son who fed Tammy, me, our family and our staff. They brought food to our home every few days and packed our freezer. When you reach out in love, don't expect anything in return. But you are going to get something in return because what you sow, you will reap.

LET GOD BE THE JUDGE

The greatest deterrent to fellowship among the Body of Christ is trying to figure out who's right and who's wrong. I almost lost my mind one time. When I hosted the 700 Club, people would come and say, "Did you know whom you had on the program?" I would say, "No, who?" Then they would say, "Well, that person is not right with God, and they did this, this, and other things." I got ulcers worrying who was right and who was wrong.

It was during that period of my life when I was very ill, I stopped at a stop light and God spoke to me. Right there God made a deal with me. He said, "Jim, you love them and I'll judge them!" I said, "God, that is the best deal I have ever heard!" I took it and I don't have ulcers anymore. I can sleep now because I can love everybody and God can judge them.

I even got so brave, a few weeks ago, I invited a Jewish man to come be my guest on PTL. He wanted to talk about the Holocaust which interests me much, for I love the Jewish people. Mr. Goldberg came and shared. We prayed together and I prayed that the God of Abraham, Isaac and Jacob would bring us together and unite us in God. A few weeks later, Mr. Goldberg said, "I can't understand it. You haven't tried to convert me yet. I have become a good friend of yours and I don't pass my friendship out to just anyone, but you all have something."

I want to share with you the conclusion of this story. We have a local radio station that makes fun of Christianity and PTL, and I want you to know that about the only person in Charlotte, North Carolina who publicly came out and spoke in behalf of PTL was Mr. Goldberg, my Jewish friend. God says, "You love them, I'll judge them." Luke 6:37 reads: "Judge not, and ye shall not be judged: condemn not, and ye shall not be condemned: forgive, and ye shall be forgiven."

If the Church of Jesus Christ and the members that profess to be a part of the Body of Christ will stop judging one another and begin to love, we are going to turn the world upside down.

Did you ever have somebody that picked out all your faults? You say your wife, your husband. 1 Corinthians 13:5 reads in the Living Bible, "Love hardly notices when others do wrong."

Many people have felt that spirituality is pious praying, pious demonstration and pious worship. Jesus had much to say about that kind of participation without love. Dr. Palmer (a great theologian), recently said on our broadcast, that after long research he has come to the conclusion that spirituality is not worship to God, but how you treat your fellow man, how you treat those around you. How important this is! 1 John 4:20 states: "If a man say, I love God, and hateth his brother, he is a liar; for he that loveth not his brother whom he hath seen, how can he love God whom he hath not seen."

LOVE IS MORE THAN WORDS

If you want to love God, love your fellow man. Love that Catholic priest, love that Protestant pastor, that nun, that sister, that worker in the other denomination. Love one another and demonstrate the love of God; because if you can't love them, how can you love a God whom you cannot see? Serving God is more than lip service.

If I was with a brother and said: "I love you, I love you, I love you, I love you, Hallelujah!" He would like that for a while but soon he would say, "Why don't you do something if you really love me?"

If I really love him, I would demonstrate that love. I would take care of his children if they were sick. He could then say, "Jim Bakker really loves me." If his wife needed help and I helped his wife, he would say, "Oh, that is a wonderful thing. He is helping my wife." In helping his family I would be demonstrating my love. It is the same way with God. If you love God, then love His family — because that is next to the heart of God. Jesus Himself declared that our demonstration of love to others was equal to doing the same for Him: "Verily I say unto you, Inasmuch as ye have done it unto one of the least of these my brethren, ye have done it unto me" (Matthew 25:40).

Love's actions speak louder than words in any relationship. Suppose Tammy and I, for example, walked together and talked together and did everything together. We just loved each other so much. Everything we did, we asked each other about it and then I got in the middle of a large crowd and all of a sudden I dropped down on my knees and loudly said, "Oh, Tammy, you are so wonderful!" What would she think?

People say, "I fellowship with God" but they only show off when they get in a prayer meeting, or they only demonstrate their love to God when they get in a crowd. Hey, where is their walk with God? Serving God is more than lip service. It is a relationship. If you have faith and you wonder why you don't get answers to prayers, let me read the answer from Galatians 5:6, "for in Jesus Christ neither circumcision availeth any thing, nor uncircumcision; but faith which worketh by love." Your faith goes into action through love.

I think of Mark Buntain, the great missionary to India, and all of the thousands of little children he has helped feed. He loves to help people in any way he can. One day he was driving down the street and saw a man waiting for a cab in the rain. So Mark Buntain stopped to pick up this man and the man said, "No, I'll catch a cab." But Mark said, "No, I want to take you where you are going." He had compassion for the man standing in the rain.

A year or two after that, Mark was trying to build a hospital in Calcutta, India. He had one more permit to obtain and was having a rough time getting approval to build the hospital. He walked into the room of the government official who could grant the last permit and guess who was sitting behind the desk? You are right. The man in the rain! God honors you when you reach out to touch others.

THE SALVATION TEST

We've shared about "Love Is Now." The Bible tells us there is a time for this, a time for that, but there is one thing God says that there is a time for now, and now is the day of salvation. "Behold, now is the accepted time, now is the day of salvation."

There are a lot of tests today on television and in national magazines. There is the National Drivers Test, The National School Test, and many others. I want to give you the International Salvation Test right now. It will tell you if you are ready for heaven — God's scriptural test for whether or not you are ready to meet God. Here it is in 1 John 4:7-9: "Beloved, let us love one another, for love is of God; and everyone that loveth is born of God, and knoweth God. He that loveth not knoweth not God; for God is love. In this was manifested the love of God toward us, because that God sent his only begotten Son into the world, that we might live through him."

Remember, as a Christian you must love because when love dies, churches split, Christians bicker, homes are divided, and people are hurt.

You can know that you have passed from death into life; the Bible says: "We know that we have passed from death into life because we love the brethren. He that loveth not his brother abideth in death."

This is God's Word. It is how you know you are saved, born again into the Body of Christ. If you are born again, Galatians 5:22-26 is for you. This is the fruit of a born-again Christian: "But the fruit of the spirit is love, joy, peace, longsuffering, gentleness, goodness, faith, meekness, temperance: against such there is no law. And they that are Christ's have crucified the flesh with the affections and lusts. If we live in the Spirit let us also walk in the Spirit. Let us not be desirous of vain glory, provoking one another, envying one another."

This is the spirit of the born-again Christian. What is the spirit of those who will not inherit eternal life, the lost? Galatians 5:19-21 taken from the Living Bible says: "But when you follow your own wrong inclinations, your lives will produce these evil results: impure thoughts, eagerness for lustful pleasure, idolatry, spiritism (that is encouraging the activities of demons), hatred and fighting, jealousy and anger, constant effort to get the best for yourself, complaints and criticisms, the feeling that everyone else is wrong except those in your own little group — and there will be wrong doctrine, envy, murder, drunkenness, wild parties, and all sort of thing. Let me tell you again as I have before, that anyone living that sort of life will not inherit the kingdom of God."

This is the fruit of the flesh and those who do such things will not inherit the kingdom of God. I trust this day if your life is not filled with the fruit of the Spirit, but the fruits of death and the flesh, that you will ask God to let you draw close to Him and become a part of the family of God. One of the problems we face today in the Church is not the world outside but the world inside — the organized church, the body or local assembly. It is so important that we, who name the name of Jesus Christ are not guilty of dividing the Body of Christ.

WHAT WOULD JESUS DO?

Recently I read an article from a newspaper in Charlottesville, Virginia. The headline read "Prayer Guides Campaign of a Born-Again Candidate." I've known this great gentleman for years, he is a car dealer in Norfolk, Virginia. He is a wonderful man and stated in this article that God had called him to run for a political office. The only group making a negative statement came from one of the largest known religious bodies in the world. They came out against him and told people to beware of anybody who professes to be a born-again Christian in politics. We see this happening time and again. Laws passed that hinder the church have been instigated because one member wanted to get back at some other religious body. But these people will someday fall into the very trap they have set for their brothers. It is so important that we reach out. We cannot control what any religious body or what any other person does but we can control what we do.

I have been asked, "Why did you invite Larry Flynt to come to the PTL Club?" Why did I love him? Why did I care? In my natural flesh I knew it could be suicide for my ministry to reach out in love to a pornographer. I put my ministry on the line because I asked the question, "What would Jesus do?" I believe if we get off our crusades and start loving people, we will win the world. It is easier to fight pornography than it is to love the pornographer!

What would happen if we would love those who are unlovely and those who are into drugs, and all the other things that we preach against?

If we would love them and win them to Jesus, we would clean up the pornography, the sin, and the lust, right at its very root. I cannot control what Larry Flynt did or will do in the future; but I can control what Jim Bakker does, and I choose to love! It is so important that the Church love the unlovely, that we love those whom we do not understand; that we love those we disagree with and we show them the love of God. Loving does not mean we condone the sin. But simply love the sinner.

In conclusion, I want to share a brief story about my brother who died when he was only 40 years old. As he lay dying, I began to remember something in his life. It was the last time he ever went into a church. In that church my father was head usher. For some reason my brother had rebelled against God, but that night my father and mother brought him back to church, and for the first time he was back in a service. During the service the offering was to be taken, and my father asked my brother to take up the offering with him since no one else was sitting in the back. Whether he was right or wrong, he felt it would be a good thing. But the wife of the pastor of the church came up quickly and took the offering plate from my brother's hands and said, "You are not fit to receive the offering." My brother never walked into another church the rest of his life.

I flew to see him a few years ago as he lay dying in the Veteran's Hospital of a rare disease. For the first time in my life, I was able to tell my brother I loved him. We had been separated so long by so much. As he lay dying, he wanted to see my cousin, Margie, the only person he knew that loved him. In his dying moments, he climbed on an airplane and flew to Pasadena. Like a dying animal in the last moment of life trying to find love, he went to her home. As she loved him and prayed with him, he accepted Jesus Christ

as his personal Savior. I had prayed for Bob all his life
and at every service I would raise my hand and say,
"pray for my brother Bob." But there in his moment of
death, he dragged his weakened body to the only person he knew that really loved him. At his death he requested that there be no funeral and I know why —
because he didn't think anyone would come. He died
alone. Oh, people, let's love and leave the judging to
God!

YOU DID IT UNTO ME

I wonder how many Christians have cried alone
because no one was there to help them during their
time of need. I wonder how many of you have fallen into sin or have had something happen in your life that
people misunderstood, and the very people that you
needed turned their back on you. Don't you be guilty
of doing the same things to others. I know what it is to
cry alone. I know what it is to be misunderstood. I
know what it is to be written about in the press. For
weeks I was lambasted in headlines. The wealth of
PTL, the wealth of Jim Bakker; and finally the audits,
which I requested myself, were completed and they
found out I was only worth $15,000. Then they turned
around and made fun of me because I didn't have
enough insurance to cover my family. Yes, maybe
your priest or pastor needs a friend, too!

"Hereby perceive we the love of God because he
laid down his life for us, and we ought to lay down our
lives for the brethren" (1 John 3:16).

"Verily, I say unto you, inasmuch as ye did it not
unto one of the least of these, you did it not to me. And
these shall go away into everlasting punishment but
the righteous into everlasting life" (Matthew 25:45-46).

Jesus was saying, "If you don't do it to those around you, if you don't love them, you're not loving me." As we close our eyes in a moment of prayer, I ask you to examine your own heart today and say, "God, if I am not loving Thee the way I should, help me now. If I am not where You want me to be, help me now to begin to love my fellow man. Help me to let Jesus Christ come through me to them. I determine to start loving now."

4 With Hope, You Can Make It Happen

Early in July 1979, God spoke to Jim Bakker to give a message on hope and encouragement to the PTL Club audience attending that day's taping. The following is that address.

If you are going to be a successful person, you have to start with a dream and put both God and yourself into that dream.

In the Gospel of John, chapter 10, Jesus proclaims, "The thief cometh not, but for to steal, and to kill, and to destroy: I am come that they might have life, and that they might have it more abundantly."

Somehow our modern thinking has managed to twist this truth around to make it appear like the opposite is true — that God is the thief, to say "no, no" to all our fun and adventure and that the worldly, sinful way is the way to really "live it up."

GOD WANTS YOUR LIFE TO BE ABUNDANT

To think that God doesn't want your life to be rich, exciting and full of adventure is the greatest lie that I know. The word, abundant, that Jesus uses here in verse ten, literally means to excel and superabound, both in quality and quantity.

God wants each of us to superabound in every part of our life. I believe that if we hold on to this exciting perspective toward life, it will always be grand, no matter what happens. Even in the midst of great turmoil, life can be an adventure.

When Tammy and I first started out together 18 years ago, we decided that we would look at every experience in our lives as an adventure. When it's 100 degrees outside, and the air conditioning is broken and everything has gone wrong, you have to look at it that way or you'll give up.

START WITH A DREAM

Believe me, if we hadn't held on to our dream, Jim and Tammy would have given up long ago. If I only had the vision of being able to do how much I could when I started, I never would have gotten off the launching pad. In fact, when I started out as an evangelist, I couldn't stay in one place very long because I only had three different sermons that I could preach.

With God's help, and keeping a vision before us, we've come a long way since then. And people seem to forget the years it's taken to get where we are now.

All the time, people come to me and say, "Jim, I

don't have any faith. Pray for me that God will give me faith." Well, my Bible says that faith is "the substance of things hoped for."

That means that faith comes when we exercise our hopes. I don't have to pray for anyone to have hope. It's simply a mental exercise. If you can dream, you can hope.

Some people have hope of heaven . . . and if that's all they want or dream about, that's all they will get. But there's a lot more blessing and abundance available if we bring our hope from way out there down to earth.

Do you want a happy home? Don't give up hope that your husband (or your wife) is going to change. Don't give up hope that you're going to have a nice house or car. Whatever your dream is, don't give it up! Remember, from our scripture in John, chapter 10, who the thief is that wants to steal our dreams.

Satan wants to steal your dream and you must resist him. If you keep that dream and that hope and read God's Word, it will build into faith. It really works!

Nearly all the faith that God has ever allowed me to exercise, started out as a dream. I saw this church (Heritage Village) in a dream. I got up out of bed and I sketched it on a piece of paper before we had land or money or anything. Then when PTL needed to expand, from the little studio in the furniture store, that dream turned into faith and I began to see a new studio building sitting on an empty field. Six months later my dream had become reality.

But it started out as a dream. I had another dream about a place where people could come from all over the world and share, pray and join together in worship as families. This dream is becoming real today in the

construction of Heritage, USA. I've held on to that
dream for years and years, and it wasn't easy.

THE DREAM STEALERS

It's amazing how many people have tried to kill
that dream. That's right, Satan will use people to try to
steal your dream. Even good, Christian people will try
to kill your dreams and try to tell you that it's not
God's will. They'll say, you shouldn't do this or you
shouldn't do that . . . But if you want to succeed, you
must let God tell you His will.

I think that the greatest thieves in all the world are
those who steal somebody's dream . . . dream
tramplers. Your dream might be just to have a new
color television set or to go on vacation. Don't give it
up. It's what keeps us alive and vital. It keeps that
adrenalin flowing and keeps us young.

On my next birthday, I'll be forty. In the past twenty years, I've lived the lifetime of maybe ten people
because I've always held on to my dreams. You can
stay young and be revitalized if you'll start dreaming
again. When you give up your dreams, a part of you
begins to stop living. That's why retirement is so
dangerous.

I was reading about how long a person lives after
they retire. The insurance companies have it all
charted out. They play the odds and can predict how
long you're going to live. They know you won't live
long after you retire unless you allow your dream
machine to stay alive and active and continue living
out your dreams.

KEEP ANTICIPATING

People in nursing homes and rest homes deteriorate so rapidly because they feel trapped and unable to get out. There is no outlet to either spark or live out their dreams so they die. When I go to rest homes, I try to tell the people to stay mentally active: go for a ride, get out even if it is just a walk across the lawn, but keep anticipating.

I like what an elderly man told me: "I'm going to live until I die." That's what my grandmother did. She had so much spunk that she lived until she was 89 and never did go to a hospital. She told us. "If you ever take me to a hospital, I pray I'll die as you carry me out of the house." She wanted to live where she was useful and she did just that.

Our minds are so powerful. We were created in the image of God and if we ever discover how much power we have in our heads, and do not give it to God, we'll be dangerous. I believe we're just beginning to understand the potential of the mind. You can control your whole body by your brain. The organs of your body can heal or die by your mental attitude. People with definite mind power can actually slow their hearts down and tell their hearts to stop beating so fast. That is why the Bible tells us that as a man thinks, that's what he's going to be.

SUCCESS IS AN ATTITUDE

My dad has always had an attitude of health and it's paid off. In the 40 years that my Dad worked, I don't think he ever took a day off for sickness. He and my Mom had that determination and now they're in their seventies and still going strong because mentally they have not stopped. They are here at the PTL Club everyday and at the evening services almost every night.

Today there are young people who are mentally dead. You might as well bury them because they've given up their dream and are only existing.

Jesus came to make our lives superabound. I want you to hope and dream. Ladies, maybe you see a beautiful hat or dress that is more than your budget. Don't quit dreaming about that thing. It doesn't hurt to start small in your dreams. When I started as an evangelist, I believed God for $50 a week . . . Now I have to believe God for a million dollars a week.

However, I would have never gotten to a million dollars if I'd refused the $50 faith. A lot of people hear great stories of faith (even on PTL) and want to jump right in at a million dollar level and then they complain, "Why doesn't God do this for me?" They want God to take them right out of kindergarten into college.

THE SCHOOL OF FAITH

There's a school of faith that we must go through. And it is never too late to start. Recently, I had a guest on the program who decided to be a missionary when she was in her 60's. Now she's off in Africa building churches.

This is what our vision for a refirement (not retirement) community at Heritage USA is all about. It's going to be a place where people practice their dreams and hopes instead of sitting around complaining about what they can't do.

Whether you are young or old, the day you accept the fact that you can put your dreams into practice is the day you'll discover you can do all things through Christ. You can, you know. It is not my word — but

God's promise in Philippians 4:13.

I have a saying among my staff which capsulizes this. Most of our people accept it and it's called, "make it happen." If it's your dream and God's will, then get in there and make it happen. It's not going to happen by itself.

Ask a farmer how much he can pray to make his fields grow by themselves. That farmer has to make it happen. He has to go out and get on his tractor and plow his fields. Then he has to plant and cultivate before he can have a harvest.

Now if God's blessing wasn't there, it would never happen. But God is not going to do it all supernaturally for us. He gives us the sunshine and rain and the knowledge and ingredients to make it grow, but there's also our part.

What has happened at PTL, the growth, etc., is supernatural. But it never could have happened if all the Partners hadn't given and my staff hadn't worked so diligently. If I never asked for help or believed to do more, we still wouldn't be off the launching pad.

People sometimes write me and say, "Jim, why don't you just have faith and not ask for anything?" I've found those people are the ones that have never done one thing. They say, "Oh, Jim, I'm living by faith." But they are living in a grubby shack and not doing anything to help anyone.

Faith without works is dead. And my God does not sponsor lazy kids. If you are going to be an overcoming child of the King, God wants you to go out and do battle and gain the victory in the name of Jesus. We are children of the Lord of the Harvest.

When hope is really restored in the Body of Christ and we put it into action, watch out. Already, the army of the Lord is coming together. There's a lot of preparation going on. Today, you may be going through something that's not pleasant, but God is the master planner. He may be stretching your vessel to receive more. And don't forget, He has come to make your life excel, to cause it to superabound with life and love.

Hold on to your dreams today. God has a great tomorrow and a greater eternity awaiting us.

5 Move In God's Timing

In May 1978, Jim Bakker gave the following message as speaker for the Greater Pittsburgh Charismatic Conference held at the Civic Auditorium in Pittsburgh.

The Bible says in Ecclesiastes, chapter three that there's a time for everything. Starting in verse one: "To everything there is a season and a time to every purpose under the heaven: A time to be born, and a time to die; a time to plant, and a time to pluck up that which is planted; A time to kill, and a time to heal; a time to break down, and a time to build up; a time to weep, and a time to laugh; a time to mourn, and a time to dance; A time to cast away stones, and a time to gather stones together; a time to embrace, and a time to refrain from embracing; a time to get, and a time to lose; a time to keep, and a time to cast away; a time to rend, and a time to sew; a time to keep silence, and a time to speak; a time to love, and a time to hate; a time of war, and a time of peace."

Let us pray.

Heavenly Father, I pray in the name of Jesus Christ of Nazareth, that you'll be with us in this moment. God, anoint these words with the Holy Spirit so that people will have their lives changed — more than just feel your presence...and they will act upon your message and go forth and be new creatures doing exploits in faith in the name of Jesus. Amen.

The message that I now want to share is, "How to Be Successful By Moving in God's Time or Timing." This is a message that has burned in my heart for months. I've tried to share it twice before but only now as I was praying did the Lord speak to my heart and say, "Now is the time!"

The key to the growth of the PTL ministry came when God showed me the big three mountain-moving principles: TRUST, DELIGHT and COMMIT from Psalms 37. They have so radically changed my life, I've written a book about it.

God promises that when you trust and delight in Him, He'll give you the desires of your heart. You first trust God and He will feed and care for you. Then you commit your way to Him and He will bring it to pass. *Anything* you commit to God, He will bring it to pass. That is powerful!

I began to act on that promise and mountains began to move. Not just for me but for others, too. Some people took these principles which God showed me and they were trying to apply them and weren't getting results. They would come to me and say, "Jim, it really isn't working for me. How come God doesn't do those things I want Him to, like He's doing in your life?"

I asked God, "Why?" And He said, "Because they are moving in their own time. If they will move in My time and wait, I will move their mountains."

GOD'S COUNTDOWN FOR HIS CHURCH

There is a timing for everything — including the Church of Jesus Christ. Just days ago, I stepped before a gathering in a giant stadium of nearly sixty thousand people, Protestants and Catholics all together, worshipping Jesus. The press couldn't believe it. They asked, "Mr. Bakker, what in the world is happening?"

I replied, "This is a wedding rehearsal. The bride is being prepared." The Church of Jesus Christ is in God's time plan and the final countdown has begun. One of these days soon the heavens are going to open and our Savior is going to be there in those clouds and we're going to rise to meet Him in the air.

In God's countdown of these last days, Jesus is getting His Church ready. And He wants to use you. The raptured Church is not going to go out defeated, whimpering, weak and mamby-pamby; the Church is going to leave this world unified and triumphant. The enemies of the Church are going to fall left and right and wonder why they cannot defeat the army of God. But the power of the Holy Spirit is undergirding the Church today so that we *are* successful and are rising triumphant under His anointing.

All around I hear of gloom and doom, and it's true, we live in perilous times. But I have yet to see a loving bridegroom that would beat up the bride the day

before the wedding! You are a gift of God and He
delights in and wants to use you.

EVERYONE WILL BE USED

How and who will be used of God today? We read
in Acts 2:17 and 18 from the Living Bible, " 'In the last
days,' God said, 'I will pour out my Holy Spirit upon *all*
mankind, and your sons and daughters shall prophesy, and your young men shall see visions, and your
old men dream dreams. Yes, the Holy Spirit shall
come upon *all* my servants, men and women alike,
and they shall prophesy.' "

This is a glorious day! Everyone can be used of
God — the young, the old, men and women.

For a long time, people thought that women
shouldn't do anything in the church. It is decent and in
Biblical order for God to use women to prophesy and
be used of God. In our own ministry, we have about
ninety husband and wife teams that work for PTL.
The world says that husbands and wives shouldn't
work together in the same business. But we don't live
by the world's standards. We go by the Bible's standards. We have many women who are moving up in
the ministry. Why? Because God is pouring out His
Spirit, His anointing, on *all, all* flesh — including *you*.

THE OLD DREAM DREAMS

Some of you will say, "but I'm too old." Oh, no
you're not. It says here that old men shall dream
dreams. Come on, old man. Let's dream some dreams.
Look at Corrie Ten Boom. She was active when most
people her age were in the rest homes, and she did

more in the last ten years than most people do in their lifetime. Consider Dr. Norman Vincent Peale, who is in his eighties. He was on PTL the other day, and he has God's Spirit upon him. His main goal in life is to see every member of his congregation and all he reaches to be born-again. He's not getting older, he's getting better.

A dear Greek lady came on the program stating she had received a call from God to go on the mission field when she was 63. Her friends said she was crazy; she should be in her rocker. But she dreamed a dream and lived in that vision. Nobody would sponsor her, but she knew in her heart that God had called her to go. And you know what's happened?

Now in her seventies, she has gone to Africa. She hasn't built just one church, she went in and built two beautiful cathedrals. She raised the money singlehandedly because men wouldn't help her.

How did she do it? She asked God for a miracle even though she was in her sixties. God then began to give her a talent in creative art. She had never painted before, but she started to paint these rare, beautiful artworks in the Greek church called Byzantine icons. And now she sells her artworks for thousands of dollars.

No one would help her, so like a little red hen, she went to work and built the church herself as God gave her the talent.

THE YOUNG FULFILL VISIONS

You're never too old or too young, either. The Bible talks about young people, and this is surely a day when God is not leaving out the young people. Just look around. Evie Tornquist, the number one sacred music artist in America today, began recording when she was just a little girl; she made her first major record when she was 13 years old.

Young people are suddenly coming into the limelight. Debbie Boone has had one of the best selling hit records in history. The Humbard kids are all being used of the Lord. If it wasn't for youth, we could never have built the PTL Television network. That's because if you had experience, you would have never dared to go into an operation like PTL. But God gave the young people a vision. Our camera men, our directors and artists didn't know a lot about TV when they started, but they were willing to work hard and learn because they had a vision.

Not long ago, the PTL Television Network was just a dream in the hearts of a small group of us. We had lost everything we had except our vision and our faith in God. With only a few dollars between us, our young people began to design remote trucks and studios. Today we have a multimillion dollar remote truck that can televise the broadcasts on location to millions around the country.

We've seen PTL grow from zero until today *Variety* magazine says, "The PTL Club is now the most watched daily TV program in the world." When we started in Charlotte, our budget was $20,000 a month. I thought then, how can we ever have enough money to stay on the air on just one station? Today, the Network is going via satellite 24 hours a day, going to city after city to over 200 regular broadcast stations and thousands of cable systems with a million dollar a week budget.

If you will live in your vision, God will bring it to pass.

WEAKNESS IS NO HINDERANCE

Some of you will say, "But Jim, I'm so weak. Can God use me?" God delights in using weak people. I believe that each one of us has a weakness. Maybe yours is a tendency to gossip. Or, maybe you've had a problem with nicotine or alcohol and still have to fight to hold it under.

So let's be honest. As the bumper sticker says, "Christians are not perfect, they're just forgiven." It's about time ministers and churches and religious groups stopped putting on the phony front that says everything is perfect when you have Christ. It's not. We still have a bunch of problems, maybe even more, but we've got a God to solve them for us one at a time. That's the difference!

I have a hard time relating to people who fly two feet off the ground and never have problems. There's something phony somewhere. Even the Apostle Paul had a thorn in the flesh that kept him humble. In my own life there have been problems that I've asked God to remove and heard His loving response, "I'm going to let you live with that thing because I want to use you and let people know Jim Bakker is not perfect or any sort of God."

DON'T CAMP AT YOUR PROBLEM

God will use you with your problems — as long as you don't camp at them. Satan wants to smash your dreams with those problems and some of you have let him. Some of you are like the family who up north in the middle of the winter blizzards dreams of sunshine and warmth. So they pack up and head for Florida. On the way, they run into a detour and on the detour, the road gets muddy and they get stuck. Instead of figuring and working a way out, they pull out the lawn chairs and camp out in the middle of the mud hole and never get to their dream.

You can laugh at that, but a lot of you let the devil rob you of your goal and vision. Even now you may be mired down at a detour. To you, the Bible says, "I can do all things through Christ which strengtheneth me." Now, the Bible doesn't say, "all things today." There is a timing with God. If you live in your vision, God will work "all things together for good" — even the detour, the muddy road, the problem.

God tests us to get us to choose the good. If it is good, if it is God, it will last. Tammy sings a song, and it says "the world didn't give it to me and the world can't take it away." They can take your car or maybe your house, but they can't take God or your faith. No matter what you go through, if you keep God and your faith, you can rebuild bigger and stronger than before. Nobody gives up anything for God that God doesn't give them back something bigger and better.

So don't say you're too weak. When God is through with you, your weakness will be your strength. This is what Paul said. In God's timing, he will use everyone — the old, the young, the weak and the strong.

THE RIGHT TIME TO MOVE

As we've read from Ecclesiastes, "everything is appropriate in its own time." That's because, though God has planted eternity in the hearts of men, men cannot see the whole scope of God's work from beginning to end. We don't see the whole picture, so we don't always know God's time. We can move out of

God's time and mess things up.

Do you know there is a wrong time to ask your boss for a raise? I learned the hard way. You don't go in to your boss for a raise when the operation is falling apart, and there's no money for anything. If you want your raise, wait until his wife has treated him good that day, until the stock is up and the operation is running smooth. Then when he's in a good mood, you'll get it with the proper timing.

I've been in prayer services where people have pushed and shoved and practically knocked people down in order to get to the front of a healing line.

I've never seen one of those shoving people get healed. They weren't willing to wait on the Spirit of God to move. They didn't heed God's word which says, "Humble yourselves, therefore, under the mighty hand of God that He may exalt you *in due* time."

Dr. Claire Weeks wrote a book on the nervous system which blessed me immensely during a difficult period in my life. I had let the pressures of the world come upon me. One of her key points for healing the nervous system was to let time pass. That truth is capsulized in this saying: "Time heals all wounds," and its reverse: "Time wounds all heels."

My problem and a lot of other people's was the latter. You think somebody in the church has hurt you or got by with a dirty deal and it bothers you. Well, I've learned that all you need to do is wait. Don't lift a finger, God in time will reward them justly. You may feel someone is keeping you from God's plan for you. If they are, God will move them out of the way in due time. He will take care of the situation.

OBSTACLES CAN BE GOD'S DELAYS

Often, the obstacles that come up in the way of our
goals are God's delays to work out His timing.
Whenever we go into building projects, I pray, "God,
I'm not smart enough to do all these things, and so if
I'm doing something that *You* don't want me to do,
You stop it." God did just that when we were building
Heritage Village. Before we could get through con-
structing the building we planned, God wouldn't let
me have the zoning to finish the job. I chomped at the
bit for weeks over that. But God knew there wouldn't
be room enough for all of it, so He stopped me and
used the government officials to do it. Since then, He
has given us two square miles, an entire city, Heritage
USA, on which to expand. God had a bigger plan than
I did.

God will take us highest, but He will never take us
higher if we don't first use all we have. God never lets
me build until I have used every office. I have put offices in halls and closets until God says, "Now you can
expand." Don't expect God to shoot you out in space
somewhere. Let God cause you to grow naturally.

Like trees in their season, sometimes your growth
will seem faster than others. There will be times, like
the trees in winter, when your vision seems to be dying, but if you know it's of God, never give up your
vision. Tammy used to sing that song, "I've had a vision of Jesus." One line says, "if I but live in that vision,
one day it will be swallowed in reality." If you will live
in the vision God has given you, one day it will come to
pass, for Jesus is the fulfiller of dreams. God has a
plan: "in the fullness of time, God sent . . ."

When men send a rocket ship to the moon they
must calculate the moon's path exactly. A few
seconds and inches off in trajectory can mean
thousands and thousands of miles off target when it

goes into space.

Do you see the importance of timing and the importance of waiting on God's timing, letting Him fulfill His plans in us?

GOD'S PLAN FOR US

When I went to buy furniture for Heritage Village, I went into a store and said, "I want one of those and I want three couches of that color and five of that color. I want 15 of those and 25 of those, and give me 50 chairs like that, etc." The salesmen seemed to go crazy. They said it was the biggest order in the history of the store. Some people looking on were thinking, "Who is this wild, impulsive buyer?" I wasn't, however, buying impulsively. For weeks, I researched Williamsburg furniture, going through books and catalogues. I chose the colors for each of the rooms. I had done my work ahead of time. So when the time was right, I could move, and move decisively.

When God opens a door for us, it is out of a perspective based on the knowledge and preparation of all eternity.

Many years ago when Tammy and I were just young evangelists of 18 and 21, God called us to take the gospel to Latin America. But at the time, all the doors were closed and we couldn't go. For 18 years, we waited for the right time to go to Latin America. One day on the PTL program, a missionary to Latin America was my guest and God said, "Now is the time to go to Latin America."

I reached out my hand to this man and said, "You are going to host the PTL Club in Spanish, and we're going to take the program to all of Latin America." Within weeks, we were on the air, and today we are on in almost every Spanish-speaking nation. Via the television medium, we are reaching millions more than Tammy and I could have ever done on our own. Why? Because it is God's time.

Jesus knows the perfect timing for us. When the disciples asked Him to go to a feast, He said, "I go not up yet unto this feast; for my time is not yet full come." To the church at Philadelphia in Revelation 3:8, Jesus said, "I know thy works: behold, I have set before thee an open door, and no man can shut it: for thou has a little strength, and has kept my word, and hast not denied my name."

Stay with your vision and dream. I believe every born-again Christian who would be led by the Spirit will know how and when to move in God.

Finally, there is one thing that God says you don't wait for. The Bible clearly declares, "Behold, now is the day of salvation." If you have not taken the first step of inviting Christ into your life, now is your time to come to Jesus — now is your time to get into God's plan and timetable. Then you, too, will find God preparing and molding you into this mighty army and prepared bride which shall reign with Christ through all eternity. Will you say with me, "I want to know Jesus and be in His will"?

6 Don't Quit Working

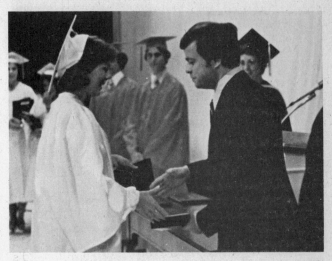

Graduation exercises for the first senior class of PTL's Heritage Academy was held on May 31, 1979. Jim Bakker challenged the eight graduating seniors in his message to students and parents.

In the book of James, chapter 2, starting at verse 14, we read: "What doth it profit, my brethren, though a man say he hath faith, and have not works? Can faith save him? If a brother or sister be naked, and destitute of daily food, And one of you say unto them, Depart in peace, be ye warmed and filled; notwithstanding ye give them not those things which are needful for the body; what doth it profit? Even so faith, if it hath not works is dead, being alone, Yea, a man may say, Thou has faith, and I have works: show me thy faith without works, and I will show thee my faith

by my works. Thou believest that there is one God;
thou doest well: the devils also believe, and tremble.
But wilt thou know, O vain man, that faith without
works is dead? Was not Abraham our father justified
by works, when he offered Isaac his son upon the
altar? Seest thou how faith wrought with his works,
and by works was faith made perfect? And the scripture was fulfilled which saith, Abraham believed God,
and it was imputed unto him for righteousness: and he
was called the Friend of God. Ye see then by works a
man is justified and not by faith only. In like manner
was not also Rahab the harlot justified by works,
when she received the messengers, and had sent them
out another way? For as the body without the spirit is
dead, so faith without works is dead also."

Let us pray:

*Heavenly Father, we ask you to bless these few
moments we have together, as these are about to take a
new step in their lives. God, I pray that Your hand will
be mightily upon them. That You will guide them. That
You will bless them. That You will anoint them. That
they'll always feel Your presence with them. That they
will be men and women of faith, and that by their
works they will demonstrate their faith to this generation. God, use them for Your glory's sake. In the name of
Jesus we pray. Amen.*

Perhaps the most pressing question on the minds
of all students is "How Can I Be A Success?" Each of
you, I'm sure wants to be a successful person —
though what you would define as a successful person
might be different from me.

To some, success means having a successful
business or a successful ministry or perhaps being a

successful parent. These things are certainly part of success, but only part. The essence of success is being in the total will of God. Success is not the goal, it is the result of living by God's ways. Being where God wants you to be and knowing you're in that place brings a contentment, satisfaction and joy that the world without Jesus will never know or understand.

This is not to say that God will do everything without our efforts. In the scripture, you have just read, verse 26 says, "for the body without the spirit is death, so faith without works is dead also." One of the most treacherous thoughts I know of is to feel that God or the world owes you a living. Be assured that the world will not hand you a living on a silver platter. There are many people who think that somehow the government ought to care for them and give them a living just because of who they are. These people will never be successful.

THE SECRET OF SUCCESS

There is a little wooden box that sits on my desk in my office which attracts a lot of attention. Written across the top of it are the words, Secret To Success. Nearly everyone who comes in opens the box to find out the answer. When they do, most people groan. For inside is written just one word . . . work.

I guess most are expecting some bit of philosophy or key to riches — instead of the simple word . . . work. Personally, I believe there are three ways to success . . . work, work and more work.

Our PTL Orchestra and Singers do a really super job! I hear as many compliments about this great group of young people as anything else at PTL. Their beautiful sound did not come just because they are beautiful people, which they are. Each one of them has beautiful talents. But first, they had to get together. They work and rehearse and rehearse and work. Somebody had to write the music; someone else had to write the words. Then somebody had to write the arrangements. Only then could they all get together and put their talents to work. Only then did harmony and beauty come forth because they worked at it together.

A saying I grew up hearing often was "anything worth having is worth working for." And it is a principle that has worked in my life.

DO YOUR BEST

During my senior year in high school, I helped out on the staff of our school yearbook. Part of the information we put in the yearbook about every senior was their ambitions or plans for the future. At that time, I was a Christian but God had not yet called me into the ministry.

This was to happen later in the year. When the information was needed, I said that my goal for life was to "be the best at whatever I do," — to be the best! I've discovered if you want to be the best at what you do, it's going to take hard work. It will take all your best efforts. But it will also have its rewards.

In Ecclesiastes 9:10, we read, "Whatsoever thy hand findeth to do, do it with all thy might; for there is no work, nor device, nor knowledge, nor wisdom, in the grave, whither thou goest." When you're dead, it's too late to work for God. There is no guarantee in the future. The time to work is now. Whatever your hand finds to do, do it with all your might — not half-heartedly, but with everything in you. Your best efforts and God can make anything happen if you work hard and have faith in Him.

SUCCESS REQUIRES FAITH

A lot of people miss out and don't work hard because they wonder whether they are dong the right thing and they sit worrying about it all the time, instead of working. This is where faith comes into the picture. I am thrilled with the way that God's teachers today have been instilling faith in our hearts — teaching us God's Word and encouraging us to put our faith into action.

Until we extend ourselves to the fullest, God will never move us. This is the wonderful thing about serving God, in that whether we're right or not, God promises to work all things together for good. Even calamity, even heartbreak, even misunderstanding, God will work out for our good and for His glory. When we work to the fullest in all we do, God will work it out.

This is what has happened at PTL as we've grown over the years. Really nothing has come easy at PTL. It may appear that way to some people on the outside because of our rapid growth. But I learned a secret early — until we fully utilize every building, everything we have, God never allows us to grow and go any further. We've had to turn closets into offices. To make room for classrooms in our school, we've had to use porches, even trams. What we've learned through this is if you want to graduate from plateau to plateau in Jesus Christ, you must fill every ounce of your potential where you are. Only then can you move on.

Automatically, God will cause you to graduate to the next level. The saddest people on earth must be

those people who have a dream but refuse to work on
their dream where they are. These are the people who
always think the grass is greener on the other side of
the fence. They in error want to expand before God
fills the area where they are now.

RICHES IN YOUR BACKYARD

Recently I read about a young man in Pennsylvania who was interested in the oil business. He
studied it inside and out, determined someday he
would strike oil and become rich. He had a friend in
Canada in the oil business and he contacted that
friend saying, "I want to come and find my fortune in
oil." The friend wrote back, suggesting he stay in
Pennsylvania until he had learned all there was to
know about oil. The young man studied more but soon
impetuously sold his farm for $833 and moved to
Canada to work with his friend in the oil business.
Shortly after he left the farm, the new owners were out
checking the pastures. Out from under an old board
came this awful gooey-looking junk into the cattle
water. You guessed it. The young man went to
Canada to find oil while one of the largest oil
discoveries in America was discovered on his farm. A
billion dollars of oil has been pumped from that $833
property.

A Massachusetts man sold his property to go mining in Wisconsin. He too had studied and thought he
would go to where the mining was the best. Shortly
after he left the farm in Massachusetts they found
silver there. One lump of silver that he had used as
part of a fence was nearly two feet square. He went to
Wisconsin to seek his mining fortune and there it was
in his backyard.

Another man out in California sold his ranch to go discover gold and on the land he sold they have mined $38 million worth of gold.

Then there is the story of Alla Afaded, the Persian who was obsessed with diamonds. Although he was a wealthy man, he so desired to find diamonds, he sold his lands, put his money together and searched everywhere for years until he ran out of money. Despondent and penniless, he finally committed suicide. Shortly afterwards, one of the most magnificent diamond mines in all of history was found in his own backyard.

The reason that all these men failed is as someone has said, "they didn't bloom where they were planted." They failed to fulfill their potential and grow out from where they were. It was always going to be the next adventure over the next hill. God wants us to do it now, to work now, to stand now. When we do this, we will see a growth that will take place naturally.

INVEST YOURSELF IN YOUR WORK

Success requires both effort and faithfulness. From the familiar parable of the talents in Matthew 25, Jesus speaks of the blessings of faithful labor, "His lord said unto him, Well done, good and faithful servant; thou has been faithful over a few things, I will make thee ruler over many things: enter thou into the joy of thy lord" (verse 23). The lord was pleased with that servant who used his money and invested it and caused it to grow. Conversely, the one who buried his talent was cast out and punished.

God wants each one of us to use what we have and invest ourselves and our talents wherever we are and wherever God leads us, fulfilling our every dream. If

God directs you to college, don't say, "I'm going to get educated." Go to give something to that college. Work wherever there is a place to work. If you like music, be active in the choirs and the chorale. If your interest is journalism, be on the college paper. Put yourself into what you do and there will always be a place for you. For there is always a place for hardworking, faithful laborers.

When I was in Bible School, there was another young man in my class with so much potential. He had a dynamic personality but he had one flaw. He would say, "I'm going to start at the top." He was determined that was where he would begin . . . right at the top. He decided he was going to be an evangelist, but not just any evangelist. He said, "I'm going to be a great evangelist, and now." You know where he is today? He has a broken marriage and is not even preaching the gospel.

If you are going to serve God, you'll probably not start at the top. You must build a foundation and grow. I remember some classmates laughing at me, saying, "Jim, I'm not going to go out there like you and take those country churches or preach those revivals to those poor people in the hills. I'm going to go out in the big crusades." You might have laughed too if you would have seen Tammy and me our first couple of years preaching the gospel. We would go back to coal mining towns with handfuls of people, preaching in churches where the love offering might be one live chicken. That didn't help much either, because Tammy would rather keep it as a pet than eat it.

Yet I went into those revivals and preached my heart out as if there were 50,000 people there. If there were ten people, I preached just as hard as if we were going out to face the mightiest crowds in America.

There was no national Christian television then. We did not start out preaching to our nation and to other nations on TV. We started preaching where God opened the doors. Where there was an opportunity, we walked through the door and then God would open another door. Fill where you are to the fullest and then you can expand. This is the principle of God.

DON'T WORRY ABOUT TOMATOES

My good friend, Dexter Yaeger, has come from obscurity to be one of the most successful businessmen in America. He has labored to pay the price of success. He told me something recently that is vital for anyone who would succeed and desire to become the best. He said, "Jim, when you become a man of leadership and begin to stick your head above the crowds, remember, you will get tomatoes. And when they throw them, don't try to throw them back, just make ketchup."

If you're doing something important, something above the level of the crowd, there will always be someone trying to stop you. When Nehemiah began to rebuild the walls of Jerusalem, the scoffers tried to stop him by every different kind of method all the time he was building.

Nehemiah learned there is a price to be paid if you want to be God's leader. God is still calling men and women who are willing to pay that price of leadership.

THE TRIALS ARE VALUABLE

In seeking to be a leader for God, one of the greatest truths I've learned is found in 1 Peter 1:7.

"That the trial of your faith being much more precious than of gold that perisheth, though it be tried with fire, might be found unto praise and honor and glory at the appearing of Jesus Christ."

God has a school of the desert. Every man of God throughout history that I've read about or met has gone through this school. The fastest way to graduate from this school is to learn to be able to praise God in everything. The children of Israel in the wilderness spent 40 years in this school and still didn't graduate because they refused to praise God. Their murmuring and complaining destroyed them. The problems you face in life, the stones thrown in your path will either destroy you (if you get under them), or you can make them stepping stones through praise to become great for God.

I challenge you to do the latter and become as Paul, who said, "I have fought a good fight, I have finished my course, I have kept the faith: Henceforth there is laid up for me a crown of righteousness, which the Lord, the righteous judge, shall give me at that day: and not to me only, but to all them also that love his appearing" (2 Timothy 4:7-8).

Let it be said also of you, "He has labored hard and fought a good fight; he has finished his course and kept the faith."

7 Know That God Will Make A Way

For the second year in a row, Jim Bakker returned to New York City, to address the interdenominational gathering of "Jesus '79," this time before 40,000 believers at Shea Stadium.

All over America and the world there is a move of the Holy Spirit that has people asking the question: What is happening?

I want you to know that this is that which the Prophet Joel spoke of in Joel 2:28-29. He said, "And it shall come to pass afterward, that I will pour out my spirit upon all flesh; and your sons and your daughters shall prophesy, your old men shall dream dreams, your young men shall see visions: And also upon the servants and upon the handmaids in those days will I pour out my spirit."

I want you to notice that no one is left out. God is reaching out to all in these days to the young and old alike. When we see this great outpouring of the Holy Spirit in the midst of great turmoil in the world, we must also ask: "What is happening?"

The Apostle Paul described what is happening today when he wrote prophetically in 2 Thessalonians 2:3: "Let no man deceive you by any means: for that day shall not come, except there come a falling away first, and that man of sin be revealed, the son of perdition."

BLESSING AND TURMOIL TOGETHER

Jesus also prophesied of today when He said in Matthew 24:9, "Then shall they deliver you up to be afflicted, and shall kill you: and ye shall be hated of all nations for my name's sake." To our question, how can there be an outpouring of the Holy Spirit and a falling away and persecution at the same time? Jesus said, "Be not dismayed when you see this situation, this is the time to look up for your redemption draweth nigh" (Luke 21:28).

Today is the greatest hour in the history of the Church. The disciples came to Jesus when they could not understand His teachings to the rich young ruler. They had given up all to follow Him and they wanted to know what would be the results of their discipleship. Jesus answered them by saying, "Verily I say unto you, There is no man that hath left house, or brethren, or sisters, or father, or mother, or wife, or children, or lands, for my sake, and the gospel's, but he shall receive a hundredfold now in this time, houses, and brethren, and sisters, and mothers and children, and lands (and listen to this) with *persecutions* and in the world to come eternal life" (Mark 10:30).

PERSECUTIONS WILL COME

What happens when problems and persecutions come? The Bible says that God will make a way of escape. As our brother, Stanley Mooneyhan, quoted earlier, "When the enemy shall come in like a flood, the spirit of the Lord will lift up a standard against him." We remember the words of Jesus recorded in Matthew 16:18, "And I say also unto thee, That thou art Peter, and upon this rock I will build my church; and the gates of hell shall not prevail against it."

Hallelujah! God will make a way of escape! Paul wrote the believers in Corinth, chapter 10, verse 13, "There hath no temptation taken you but such as is common to man: but God is faithful, who will not suffer you to be tempted above that ye are able; but will with the temptation also make a way to escape, that ye may be able to bear it."

GOD ALWAYS MAKES A WAY

God has always made a way of escape to those who love Him and serve Him. Noah found himself in the world's worst flood and God made a way of escape. Abraham was about to kill and sacrifice his only son Isaac, but God made a way of escape. Lot was abiding in the doomed cities of Sodom and Gomorrah, but God made a way of escape. Joseph was thrown into a pit and sold into slavery, but God made a way of escape. Moses came up against the Red Sea with Pharaoh's mighty army behind him and God made a way of escape. Joshua was pursued by five kings with mighty armies, but God made a way of escape. Gideon's small band came up against the countless armies of the Midianites, but God made a way of escape. David came up against the giant, Goliath, and the mighty armies of the Philistines, but God made a way of escape. Mordecai was a good man, was framed and supposed to be hung, but God made a way of escape. For Job, when all hope was gone, God made a way of escape. Daniel was thrown into the lions' den for standing up for God, but God made a way of escape. So there's still hope for you and me!

Baby Jesus was ordered to be slain with the newborn babies, but God made a way of escape. Paul and Silas landed in jail, but God made a way of escape. And I want you to know, that God is still making a way for the Body of believers, the Church of Jesus Christ. There is no weapon formed against the Church that will prosper. For our God will have a Church — our God will have a Church without spot, without wrinkle. He has already prepared our way of escape. His name is Jesus!

RESIST THE DEVIL

The enemy came into PTL like a flood last year. One of my writer friends told me that the atheist movement had labeled me the most dangerous Christian on earth. We faced grave financial problems. We faced investigations by federal government agencies. We faced erroneous news reports. And in the midst of it all, a psychic magazine predicted that the next month would be the final month for PTL and Jim Bakker. Well, I'm still here.

When the magazine made an astrology chart of me, my friends tried to keep it from me. But you know, "good news" always travels swiftly.

Someone made sure that I got the news that my doom was just around the corner. I prayed, asking God, "What shall I do?" My flesh at that point wanted to crawl under a bed and hide. I'm sure that is what the devil wanted me to do. But God by His Word told me, "Submit to me; resist the devil and he shall flee from you!"

The Lord then directed my attention to 1 Kings, chapter 18 where the prophet Elijah had come up against the prophets of Baal. Even though he was not in the majority Elijah dared to stand with God. Elijah came unto the people and said, "How long halt ye between two opinions? If the Lord be God, follow him. But if Baal, then follow him."

Elijah stuck his neck out for God. God spoke to me that he wanted me to do the same thing. The devil said, "You'll be a fool, Jim Bakker!" I had placed my entire life in the hands of God. And I was not about to turn back now.

PUTTING GOD TO THE TEST

The prophet Elijah put Baal to the test. Interestingly, Baal, according to my research is related to the sun, the moon and the stars — basically astrology. Elijah told the prophets of Baal to build an altar to their god. Then Elijah and the people of God built an altar to the God of Abraham, Isaac, and Israel. Being a gentleman, Elijah said, "You go first, Baal." The prophets of Baal cried out to their god, and they gnashed their teeth and cut themselves, and nothing happened. The altar of the prophet Baal was not consumed. Elijah mocked them saying, "Perhaps your god is busy, perhaps he's taken a walk, perhaps he is sleeping." Yet Baal didn't respond.

Then Elijah said, "It's time to build the altar of God." He was not content with the contest being even. He made it hard for the God of Abraham, Isaac and Israel. This is what he did. He said, "Fill four barrels with water and pour it on the burnt sacrifice and on the wood." Then he said, "Do it a second time!" And they did it the second time. I can see a few lukewarm church members getting nervous now, telling Elijah, "Don't get carried away." But a third time he had them bring barrels of water and pour them on the sacrifice. And the water ran down from the sacrifice and filled the trench round about.

Then Elijah cried out, "Hear me O Lord, hear me, that this people may know that thou art the Lord God." Then the fire of the Lord fell and consumed the burnt sacrifice, and the wood and the stones, and the dust, and licked up the water that was in the trench. And when all the people saw it they fell on their faces. And they said, "The Lord, He is the God!"

STICKING GOD'S NECK OUT

When I read this account in the Bible, I said, "God, what would you have me to do? You've shown me the story of Elijah." He said, "I want you to do as Elijah did and challenge the prophets of Baal and Satan." So I went on television in front of millions of people and challenged the god of astrology. I challenged the god of psychic phenomenon. I said, "If God be God, then let's follow God. And the devil will be defeated!"

I knew I had stuck my neck out. And many people thought I was a fool. But I want to share with you a secret: I did not really stick my neck out. I stuck God's neck out. The very month that the psychic magazine

predicted would be my last, more people wrote me
than any other month in my history. That very month,
more monetary support came in than any month in
the history of the PTL Television Network. More people called for prayer and salvation than any month in
our history. Praise God!

The editor of the psychic magazine was so curious
about all of this, he made a fatal mistake. He started to
watch the PTL Club. The editor that predicted my
doom called on the prayer phones and accepted Jesus
Christ as his personal Savior. He came and had din-
ner with my mother and father, and prayed the sinner's prayer again with one of my associates. (We
didn't want to take any chances; we wanted him really
saved.) Afterwards, he contacted his attorney and
said, "I am going to close down my psychic/astrology
magazine."

He shut down his magazine the very month he
said I would close down. "If God be God, then follow
God." Remember when the enemy comes in like a
flood, the Spirit of the Lord shall lift up a standard
against him. The enemy came into PTL like a flood in
every crack, in every window, in every door, but God,
like He said, lifted up a standard against him.

When we obey and trust God, He will deliver us
every time and push away the assaults of the enemy.
The day of this sharing, my financial managers in-
formed me that all of our PTL affiliates totaling nearly
700 broadcast outlets are now paid within 30 days cur-
rent. PTL's mountain of $13 million of indebtedness is
totally eradicated, one year ahead of the predictions
of the financial experts. "Greater is He that is in you
than he that is in the world."

As Joshua said in Joshua 24:15, "Choose you this
day, whom ye shall serve . . . But as for me and my

house, we shall serve the Lord!" Will you answer like Joshua? How many of you will do that? Right now, worship God with me! "As for me and my house, we will serve the God of Abraham, Isaac and Jacob. Thus saith the Lord."

8 The Church Triumphant

On August 11, 1979 over 1000 PTL Club Partners attend-ed the Charter meeting of the World Harvest Club at the Civic Center in Charlotte, North Carolina. Jim gave the following message to these people, his faithful sup-porters.

There is a mounting fear and anxiety in our nation as perhaps never before in our history. Our president has termed it a "crisis in confidence," but there is a questioning, a concern, a lack of trust in our political leaders, in our government, in our schools, in our businesses and in ourselves. People are worried about all kinds of shortages and are asking, "What can be done?"

Certainly, the problem is not isolated in America. As I have traveled outside of America, I saw the shortages, the unrest of the people even more pronounced. People everywhere are looking for some kind of answer; and there are plenty of opinions and theories around today.

However, I believe the answer to our questions and every problem we face in life is the Bible rather than in the experts. Just months ago, all the experts predicted that PTL would fall from attacks of certain people and because of some money problems; but God said, "No weapon formed against thee shall prosper." PTL has not only survived; it has thrived and grown during this time. Yes, God's Word has the answer!

The Bible says much about the days in which we are living. It tells about the perilous times we're facing. In Matthew 24, Jesus described a series of events before His Second Coming that reads like today's headlines. He talked about the earthquakes and just this week, San Francisco experienced its worst quake in 60 years. I believe that God gives warnings and I have to believe this was a warning from God to a city that has openly mocked God, taking an official stand in government to condone the same sin for which Sodom and Gomorrah were destroyed. God tells us that He will not wink at sin and look the other way forever. From the beginning, God warned that His Spirit would not always strive with sin but what a man sows, that also will he reap.

I believe we are in the hour of coming judgment and final preparation of the Church. Our history is rushing to a climax and there are a lot of people that deep down inside want to become a part of the Family of God and Body of Christ but think they can wait till the last minute. For some, the events of today are going to pass them by and it's going to be too late for them. Some will harden their hearts and as the Bible says, "they will be cut off and that without remedy."

THE BODY WILL CARE FOR ITSELF

For years I have asked God about the events of today and sought how we as His Body can be ready. What is the answer for the Church living in a world of crises? Over a period of months God gave me two answers and I didn't realize it at the time, but they were from the same scripture — Hebrews 10:25: "Not forsaking the assembling of ourselves together, as the manner of some is; but exhorting one another: and so much the more, as ye see the day approaching."

God said the answer, the security, is that My Body will take care of itself; but My people need to come together and fellowship and care more for one another in these days. Christian television is good but it is not the answer. Huge, growing churches are preaching the Word but they're not the whole answer, either. People must care down at the level of where they live.

As a member of the spiritual life committee for my particular denomination, I was asked to write down alarming trends I saw in the Body of Christ. One of those I saw was that our great churches can easily become impersonal to people's needs. People that are confused and hurting are getting lost in the crowd. What they really need are friends — people to put their arms around them and touch the hurts with love and compassion.

The other alarming trend, the great breakdown of the home and divorce, reveals the same need for closeness and communication. The same gospel that works in these great charismatic meetings must work down in the trenches, in our homes on a day-to-day level. And it will if we let it. Jesus says, "I am touched by the feelings of your infirmities." He is a friend that is closer than a brother. When you hurt, He hurts.

Our God is a God of detail and He is concerned about each thing down to the number of hairs on our head. In the scripture we just read, God says the way the Church will survive today's calamities is to fellowship and care for one another. The Living Bible says in that verse "not neglecting our church meetings." But I believe God is saying something more than our attending meetings. If we just come and sit in a pew and don't relate and minister to one another, we'll miss the fullness of what God has for the Church today.

THIS IS THE CHURCH'S HOUR

So many people are attracted to the meetings with the great healers. The sick want to be touched by the great ministers. In actuality, if the truth was published, the prayer phone ministry of PTL would probably be known as one of the great healing ministries of the world today. Our counselors are praying with people and seeing miracles every day, but I don't want to propagate our ministry that way. I prefer to be recognized only as a part of the Body of Christ because the day of the great single preacher or healer is drawing to a close.

This is the hour of the Church, the Body of Christ. God is saying to every pastor, every church member, "Be filled with the Holy Spirit." Each of us should pray for the sick and minister to one another's needs for it is the whole Church that is going to rise triumphant at His Coming!

The only way the whole Church can get prepared is if all the members minister to one another. There are only so many people that I or anyone can preach to personally and even then I can easily fail. It is a rude awakening for many in the Church to see their "preacher idols" as imperfect people just as they themselves are. No one preacher is going to do the whole job, even for his own church. Somehow, even if he could, I don't believe God would let him.

Today we are on the brink of events that require every part of the Body of Christ to join in and help. What if the government decides to pull the plug on Christian television (and there are those who now want this)? What if a power failure or shortage limits use of television to bare necessities? Who is going to come to your home to minister to you? There is only One who can — that One, of course, is JESUS.

Jesus will come in your brother or neighbor. God has always chosen to use men and women. We are all the arms and legs He's got. He's not going to use the angels to evangelize and love for He has said, "I've chosen you." In that calling, He charges us to pray for one another, to read the Bible together, to care for one another and share our needs and blessings together.

The days reveal it, the Spirit confirms it and we all know it: Jesus is coming soon! Our text scripture in Hebrews goes on to say, "as that day approaches, we must fellowship more." The Amplified Bible reads, "We must fellowship and exhort one another *more faithfully.*"

THE GATHERING OF BELIEVERS

In the midst of crises and falling away, Jesus, the Good Shepherd, is gathering together all the true believers in His flock. Do you know that we, the Church, are God's most-prized possession on earth — that we are gifts in which God delights? When we ignore or hurt one another, we are messing with a gift of God. We are precious to God but our neighbors are just as precious. Each one of us needs to discern and recognize the Body of Christ.

The hardest statement for me to hear from a Christian is for them to say, "Nobody cares." This is a poor commentary on the Body of Christ. We had better care. We *are* our brother's keeper and though we may not think we need the Body of Christ, one of these days everyone of us will need it.

I like to preach about victory. I'm not a preacher of doom and gloom, but I cannot ignore the warning of God's Word. Second Timothy 3:1 says, "This know also, in the last days perilous times shall come," and already we see them all around us. When the world leaders start talking about Armageddon and most of them don't even understand what it is, something is happening!

When I was a kid, people used to wonder what could possibly happen to cause such a monstrous war as Armageddon. Today we know the cause — the world is being strangled by the need for oil. Countries can be literally ground to a halt without oil. In our own country, if we run out of oil, it's all over.

How do you operate a 100-story skyscraper without electricity? These buildings are sealed so they have to have air conditioning and lights. Our whole automobile industry is dependent on fuel and if it dies, the economy of our whole nation is gone because so many industries are interrelated.

Can you tell me that when one nation has a stranglehold on the very substance that others need

to stay alive that there will not be war? The Bible says
that the mighty bear, Russia, will come down and that
the Arab oil will not lie untouched forever.

PROVISION IN CRISIS

With or without oil, experts are saying that infla-
tion has so escalated in our nation — that we are on a
crash course to disaster. In his book, Robert Preston
says that the results of the coming economic collapse
will be millions out of work, literal starvation, rioting
and looting that will sweep the nation. Willard
Cantelon, the great student of world finance, says the
end of the dollar is near. David Wilkerson says famine
is coming to the world in our generation and millions
will die. Dr. Paul Yurich of Stanford University confirms that as many as 20 million people will die of starvation in the coming year.

Jesus, Himself, told us that famine is a sign of the
last days. So what will you do, what will be your
security when you are faced with no job, no food and
worthless money? The Bible tells us in Proverbs 11:4
that, "Riches profit not in the day of wrath: but
righteousness delivereth from death." The wealthy
are not necessarily the ones that will make it during
the times of tribulation and hunger. In verse 28 of that
same chapter, Solomon declares, "He that trusteth in
his riches shall fall: but the righteous shall flourish as
a branch."

Some of you can remember the last depression we
had in this country. Who were the people that jumped
out of windows and committed suicide? It was those
that put all their hopes and faith in money and stocks
and bonds. When their god of money failed, they
couldn't exist.

During depression and hard times, the most fortunate are the poor. They hardly know the difference. I remember as a lad, my family, grandparents and relatives never went hungry during the depression. They had always shared food and took care of each other. The believers in our little Assembly church pitched in and there was always enough to go around.

GOD'S SECRET WEAPON

God has got a secret weapon against depression. It is the Body of Christ. One of my favorite scriptures, Psalm 37:3, declares that if we trust in the Lord, "verily, thou shall be *fed.*" At the bottom line, food is what it takes to survive. During the coming days, the Church of Jesus Christ will not wring its hands, worrying about what is going to happen. Rather the Church is going to rise up triumphant as the day of redemption draws near.

My personal belief is that the Church is going to escape the main onslaught of coming tribulation. When God said to "Pray that you might be counted worthy to escape these things," I believe He meant just that. I have good friends in the ministry who believe the Church will go through the tribulation and I respect their beliefs, but I cannot see God pouring out His wrath on His bride just before the marriage feast.

Whether you believe in pre-trib, post-trib, mid-trib, or pan-trib (it will all pan out), we are all going to soon find out what God has in store. God surely has the days and the times in His control but we must heed the warning of the Bible. It was a little widow woman that God sent to Elijah to feed him during the time of famine in his day and God is going to use the widow women and the whole Body of Christ as your provision in the coming days. When the bottom falls out, you may need the help and knowledge of the older people who know how to garden and farm and sew.

This is not a message of discouragement but it is Bible and God's word for *now* — that God's people must come together and care and help one another. The true New Testament Church is a loving and caring Body of believers.

If the Church today was really doing all it could, there would be no need for welfare in America. The needs of the congregation would be administered in a spirit of love and the orphans and widows would be cared for as God says they should. Instead, we've given the government more and more control until we've got a monster that has shifted our dependence on God over to man.

The New Testament Church cared and shared. Acts 2:44-46 records: "And all that believed were together, and had all things common. And sold their possessions and goods, and parted them to all men, as every man had need. And they, continuing daily with one accord in the temple, and breaking bread from house to house, did eat their meat with gladness and singleness of heart."

We may need this same New Testament formula in the Church today if Jesus tarries, and that could be a blessing. While we need individual motivation and responsibility, I don't believe God ever intended us to live such high-geared lives with so much pressure to perform and produce. This is why so many today are having nervous breakdowns. Rather God says that we are to cast our care on Him and rest in Him.

The carnal man could never equally share and Work together without destroying one another. But motivated by love, the Church *can* according to 1 Corinthians 12:25-26: "That there should be no schism in the body; but that the members should have the same care for one another. And whether one member suffer, all the members suffer with it; or one member be honored, all the members rejoice with it."

While the carnal man would get jealous with others who are blessed, we should take others' blessings in the Body as being our own family blessed; and when someone hurts, we can share that hurt by listening, consoling and loving. If we all really cared for one another like this, I believe the Church would win millions overnight.

Today, with homosexuality rampant, the devil has most of us even afraid to express our love for one another in the Body. People are dying for lack of love and friendship; and we must not let the smokescreen, the counterfeit of Satan, keep us from attending to the real needs in our church.

Jesus declared in Mark 12:31 that we should love our neighbor as ourself. This is why Tammy and I have recently dedicated ourselves to helping others personally. We, of course, will continue to minister to the masses on television, but we recognize the need to touch people individually. We have some dear friends on the verge of divorce, and I have pledged to them before God that I am going to work, talk, pray, love and listen to help keep them together.

How many of us as Christians have sat back and seen some marriage ruined in the Church and not lifted a finger? We have seen a pastor get in trouble and when it happens, instead of helping, we point the finger and condemn. The biggest indictment against the Church today is that we "kill our wounded."

This must not happen! Jesus came to heal the brokenhearted and bind up the bruised. God, today, wants each of us to befriend and help the bruised and wounded among us — to give them the "wine and oil of the Holy Spirit," that they may be restored in soul and body.

The *whole* Church in these days is going to nourish and take care of each other. That means we all have a part, a job to do. For we'll all rise together in that soon triumphant meeting with our Lord in the air. Let us all be ready for that great day!

Epilogue

A primary prerequisite for success is coming into a daily, living relationship with the Creator God, the Lord of all Creation, the Author and Finisher of our Faith. You can do this now by inviting Jesus Christ to come into your heart (the center of your life) as your Savior and Lord.

First, acknowledge that God does love and care for you and that He has a plan for your life. Jesus declares to you:

> *"I am come that they might have life, and that they might have it more abundantly."*
>
> *(John 10:10b)*

Second, confess to God that without Him you have sinned and fallen short of God's best for your life. The Bible says that indeed all of us have sinned:

> *"For all have sinned and come short of the glory of God."*
>
> *(Romans 3:23)*

Third, believe the truth that God sent Jesus Christ to pay the penalty for your sin and to be your redeemer to life eternal. The Bible declares:

> *"For God so loved the world, that he gave his only begotten Son, that whosoever believeth in him should not perish, but have everlasting life."*
>
> *(John 3:16)*

And again:

> *"And he (Jesus Christ) is the propitiation for our*

> *sins: and not for ours only, but also for the sins of the whole world."*
>
> *(1 John 2:2)*

And again:

> *"Jesus saith unto him, I am the way, the truth, and the life: no man cometh unto the Father, but by me."*
>
> *(John 14:6)*

And again:

> *"Neither is there salvation in any other: for there is none other name (Jesus Christ) under heaven given among men, whereby we must be saved."*
>
> *(Acts 4:12)*

Fourth, verbally invite Jesus into your life to be your Savior and Lord. Jesus awaits your invitation now:

> *"Behold, I stand at the door, and knock: if any man hear my voice, and open the door (of your heart), I will come in to him, and will sup with him, and he with me."*
>
> *(Revelation 3:20)*

Say this to God, using these words or your own:

"I understand that I am a sinner, and not able to reach You, God. But I believe that Jesus is Your Son and that I can come to know You through His name. I accept Jesus now into my heart as my personal Savior and Lord and begin a new life of faith never to end."

Fifth, act with assurance. The Bible promises that through Christ, we are God's sons:

> *"But as many as received him,(Jesus Christ), to them gave he power to become the sons of God, even to them that believe on his name."*
> *(John 1:12)*

...that we can have assurance of salvation:

> *"That if thou shalt confess with thy mouth the Lord Jesus, and shalt believe in thine heart that God hath raised him from the dead, thou shalt be saved."*
> *(Romans 10:9)*

...and that we should fellowship with other believers:

> *"Not forsaking the assembling of ourselves together, as the manner of some is; but exhorting one another; and so much the more, as ye see the day approaching."*
> *(Hebrews 10:25)*

If you have just made a decision to trust Christ as your Savior, I want you to write me and I'll send some literature to help you grow spiritually.

God bless you,

Jim Bakker

Enclose This Coupon In Your Letter:

Name _____

Address _____

City/State/Zip _____

Jim, please send me the booklet "Salvation, Clear and Plain" and enroll me in your Bible Study Course. Your book, "Eight Keys to Success" helped me.

Send to: Jim Bakker
                Charlotte, NC 28279